Dating Successfully – The Rules of Navigating Your Love with Your Partner

Love Never Finds You When You Are Looking for It. It Hits You Right in the Chest When You Are Least Expecting It.

The Secrets to Catching Your Love's Attention and Making Them Yours

By Lita Caine

Dating Successfully – The Rules of Navigating Your Love with Your Partner

This guide will teach you how to step into the dating pool and make the best start in your relationship.

The start of a relationship is quite delicate. Since both partners are testing the waters and navigating the complicated maze of boundaries and emotions, finding your place can be confusing. The dating rules are different for men and women. It's the feminine charm of a woman that attracts a man and vice versa when it comes to chivalry. There are certain points in every person's mind, which they want in their partner. However, your soulmate is not just roaming around waiting for you. You have got to put in the effort!

To find "the ONE," which will be a long and difficult journey, you will need to give your best. You might encounter a few bumps on the road… that's just how the process goes but when the path ends, you have to pave your own way to start your story.

How to do that is what this eBook will teach you. Follow the dating guidelines to understand how a simple date can turn into something so much more. You never know — you might be sitting across from your soulmate and making light chit-chat when there's potential to become a power couple.

Table of Contents

Introduction

It was the summer of '98 when I saw him for the first time. Our eyes met on the beach, where I was sunbathing and reading my paperback novel with a steamy cover and he was standing with his friends looking for an empty spot to set up camp.

It was me who made the first move by giving him a small smile and shifting my attention back to my novel. I had never in my life made such a bold move so to say there were butterflies in my stomach would be an understatement. After an hour or so, I felt a shadow over me. As I raised my eyes up, I saw the same guy standing right next to me.

He waved an awkward "Hi" to me and said, *"So, I noticed that you have been reading this book for quite a long time. I am pretty sure that it must be one heck of a story but would you like to join me and my friends?"*

His words took me by surprise because I hadn't thought he would ask me to join his group. Oddly, it made me feel safe. Never had anyone approached me in such a manner. So, I went over to his blanket and we had a great time. As we were packing up, he approached me and said, *"So, at the risk of sounding too forward, I do believe that you had a great time. Would you like to go on a date with me?"*

That was the beginning of our relationship and every day since then, we have worked hard to keep that special bond between us.

Have you ever had such an encounter? Have your eyes ever connected with someone, causing you to feel as if electricity shot through you? How would you best describe your emotions after meeting someone that you are attracted to?

We have got one for you:

Have we hit the right nerve? We are pretty sure we have!

Now that we have the rhythm going, let's get to the heart of the matter… What is dating all about?

Bet you never saw this question coming, did you?

The Definition of Dating

Every person has a different definition of dating and it all comes down to the generation gap. Typically, dating is defined as two people having an intimate relationship. In most cases, the relationship starts simple and then develops a sexual element, after which people search for compatibility to move forward.

As the relationship proceeds, the most important thing to focus on is to make sure that you and your partner are on the same page. This is why you need to be familiar with the basics of dating.

Different qualities can attract you to a person physically, intellectually, emotionally, or otherwise. It's easy to get lost in the excitement of your first relationship and when your rational thoughts are no longer in control of you, things don't proceed the way you had them in mind.

There's a spectrum for each relationship, which starts from healthy and when not paid attention, turns unhealthy and in some cases, even abusive. So, spot the red flags. These refer to your partner's mannerisms, which you find unacceptable.

For example, a girl is going on her first date. After a week of chatting online, the plan is to meet the guy at the restaurant, have a meal, and then see where the night takes them. She enters the restaurant and spots the guy sitting at the corner table. They exchange pleasantries and then both take their seats. A few minutes into the conversation the guy says, "You would look so much hotter if you dressed a little differently." Of course, no girl likes to hear such a backhanded compliment. Her mind made up, the girl finishes her meal quickly and takes her to leave.

Let's turn the tables and look at another situation from the guy's perspective. A girl meets a guy on an online dating app and is impressed by his clothing and face. After chatting for a while, they both decide to meet at a coffee shop. As the girl is waiting at the table for the guy, she sees him getting out of an old, rusty Chevrolet. She can't match the handsome, well-dressed guy she saw online with the guy coming towards her. Her mind made up, she decides to cut the date short to 15 minutes, fake an emergency, and leave immediately.

In both scenarios, the first impression, which was made on chat, did not hold up when the girl and guy met face to face. These are the starting red flags you should not ignore. There's no way that such a relationship has a chance of surviving because both of them couldn't connect on any level.

So, what are the points you should look for?

- Does the person respect you?
- Does the person acknowledge that you are an independent individual?
- The person doesn't argue with you on simple things or try to mansplain during a conversation
- The person is honest is with you (Although this isn't something you can be sure on when you are in the initial stages of dating; however, if they try to backtrack on something they said then the element of honesty is lost)
- The person isn't jealous of your friends or restricts you from meeting them
- Are you able to say something to the person without the fear of being judged?

Let's say that your partner does none of the things above. There's a connection between you two and your argument with yourself is, "At least my partner isn't abusive."

No, just NO!

You might have not noticed the signs but your partner might be or is abusive. Your relationship isn't healthy if:

- Your partner is distrustful, disrespectful, and inconsiderate
- Your partner doesn't openly communicate their feelings
- Your partner likes to humiliate you in social gatherings
- You feel your partner is trying to isolate you emotionally
- Your partner threatens you during arguments that they will reveal your information to your family
- Your partner doesn't like you working

These are major things that make or break a relationship before it has even begun.

The bottom line is that if you don't get comfortable vibes in the first meeting then taking anything further will put this seed of doubt in your mind that you and the person are not compatible.

Dating Rules

Who said dating was easy? If you have watched "How to Lose a Guy in 10 Days" then you know what lengths you need to go to give the other person the signal that you like them. Long gone are the days when simply saying, "I like you" worked quite well. Today, you need to go big or go home.

First dates are always awkward, second dates can be considered experimental because you are trying to figure out if you are making the right decision or not. The dates that follow after that are where you truly get down to the business of knowing each other. At this stage, you can make many mistakes, blunders, faux pas, and missteps.

We could mention some of them right now that make way for these opportunities, such as calling too often, being too available, ghosting every now and then, laughing hysterically, wearing the wrong outfit to a fancy restaurant, and committing dating crimes like chewing too loudly, telling bad jokes, checking your cell phone after every few minutes, ordering cheap so that you can pay the bill all by yourself, etc.

To avoid these, think of dating as a game. There are certain rules you need to follow so that you don't get blocked. You need to study the baselines so that when a low ball comes at you, you can easily deflect it and maintain your dignity.

For starters, let's take a look at the dos and don'ts of dating so that you don't build any unrealistic expectations in your mind.

Dos and Don'ts of Dating

Dating Dos

Do date a person you like. You are probably thinking that this is an obvious "do" but wait till you enter the dating game. There are plenty of fishes in the sea and just because you caught one, doesn't mean you have to reel it in. By that we mean if you are connected with someone on a dating app, don't agree to go on a date until and unless you don't form a bond with them. If the conversation is lacking spark when exchanging messages then chances are that you won't have much to talk about when face to face. That will be one awkward date!

Do dress your best and always be punctual. Looking messy, and saying the cliché line, "I got stuck in traffic" does not make for a good impression. This tells the person that you don't care and if that's the case then why agree to the date in the first place.

Do compliment your date the moment you see them. Men and women both put a lot of effort into getting ready for their first date because they want the other person's eyes to widen in wonderment. It truly pays off for the time you spend in front of the mirror.

Do make the best of your date. The number one rule of going on a date is you need to make up your mind that you will have fun. Yes, finding a soul mate is a serious business but the reason why your heart is beating so fast and you are feeling scared is because you are afraid of what will happen.

Do act interested in what your partner is saying. Also, look for signs if your conversation is boring them. Start with simple questions to find out which one they respond to more animatedly and then lead with that. Also, pay attention to the basic information such as their likes and dislikes, what they are ready, what kind of music they listen to, when is their birthday, etc.

Do stay positive even when your date does not go well. Let's assume that your first date didn't involve any sparks or any illuminating conversation. That doesn't mean that you give up on dating. You will have to kiss a lot of frogs before you find your prince charming. You will probably meet a few nice people along the way but if you can't form a connection with them then don't force it. Before a simple meet-up turns into a scenario where you try to come up with ideas to friend zone the person, we suggest that you end it.

Do plan ahead… yes, even on a date! Whether it's your first date or third, you need to mentally prepare yourself. Have a bunch of questions prepared to ask or you might find yourself playing with your napkin. Do not; under any circumstances, tell a joke if you are not a funny person. There's nothing more cringey than telling a joke that meets dead silence.

Do connect with like-minded people. They say that opposites attract but when your opinions don't match with the other person's opinions then it creates a huge rift, which results in a first bad impression. Moreover, in the long run, there's no knowing how long your relationship will last with the differences.

Do ask questions. Listening is one of the biggest traits a date can look forward to. Don't be the person who keeps interrupting in the middle of the story to make a point or tell your own similar story. However, do ask follow-up questions because it shows that you were paying attention to every word your date was saying.

Do offer to pay the bill. Some women believe that it's basic dating etiquette for a man to pay the bill. Let us ask you this — you both work for a living then how come it's expected from the man to pay for the food? Yes, the man will offer to pay but a woman should also offer the same, and when she does, the bill should be either split in half or both of them should pay for what they ate.

Dating Don'ts

Don't be overly persistent. How would you feel if someone, you just met, started calling, texting, and emailing you after a single date? This screams desperation! This is a major turnoff that will make you look crazier than your ex. So, put down the phone if they didn't call you. That's a major hint that they didn't feel any attraction.

Don't go for the same old. Yes, girls are attracted to bad boys and boys are more into chicks that are a little bit crazy and adventurous. Not that we are generalizing preferences. We are simply trying to explain the norms of dating that today's society has. Don't let the crazy back into your life, when you just got out of a bad relationship. It's time to break the pattern and seek out someone healthy.

Don't ever be late! Tardiness is not something that's taken lightly on the first date. Need we tell you the etiquettes of dating? You only need to remember one and that is "no ghosting." If you have changed your plans or probably will later then tell your date as early as possible. Whether you no longer want to continue with the date or have an emergency, remember to apologize... profusely.

Don't talk about your past! This is one of the biggest don'ts of dating. Let's say you are on a date and talking about something random when you see a cat dart by the table. The sight immediately reminds you of your cat, which you and your ex-partner adopted together. When the relationship ended, your partner took the cat saying that they were the ones who took care of it. Since your mind was focused somewhere else, you missed what your date was talking about. You then start to talk about bad dates in general and a rant ensues on how your last partner took the cat. The next 30 minutes are spent talking on this topic. If you had looked closely at your date then you would have realized that they were bored out of their mind. Can you picture it?

Don't lie to your date about personal things. Whether you are fibbing or hiding the truth, starting a relationship on a note where you are not honest with the person means that you are not comfortable. There's no point in pursuing the person after the date is over because you just lied to them. No matter how life-changing, silly or awful the truth is, lay it out there so that your date can decide for itself.

Don't talk too much about yourself. When it comes to dating, the name of the game is "mystery." You gotta have some so that the other person finds you interesting. If you reveal everything about yourself on the first date then they will form an impression of you. Plus, getting to know someone should be a long and fun process. That is what makes dating exciting.

Don't check out other people on your date. That's just tacky and rude. Even if you have moves that are as subtle as a ninja, trust us when we say this — the date sees it all. Give your complete attention to them and see how things go. If you don't feel the spark, follow the etiquettes of dating, which is fake a call and run for your life. Just kidding! Simply cut the date short by doing small talk and then ask for the check.

Don't get drunk on your date. For the love of God, don't start pounding hard liquor on your date. It will show your date that you have absolutely no manners and will probably try to grab them on the way home.

Don't give out personal information on the first date. You have no idea what kind of person your date is. They could be a serial killer or a child molester, disguised as a boring 9 to 5 office worker. In the case of women, never leave the cell phone behind or silence it. In the case of men, see their eyes because that's where the crazy lies. If they start talking about going to a wedding together then they are most definitely clingy. The traits differ from person to person so you need to go with your gut feeling.

Don't have sex on the first date. Love lasts longer than last and if you are attracted to a person, your body and heart will tell you to go all in. However, if you listen to your head then it will tell you that it's too early.

Don't use cheesy pick-up lines. Cheesy pick-up lines speak out loud that you are a player! It will make your date rethink your decision to meet up with you and then everything will go downhill from there.

Online dating is quite competitive, which is why it's important to be your authentic self. If you keep pretending the entire time then your date will be attracted to the new persona you have created and not the actual you. So, make sure that your words are clear and honest, listen with open ears and heart, and make eye contact to show that you are interested.

Stages of Dating

"I know I have a soul mate out there somewhere. We just have to meet."

Have this kind of thinking and you will enjoy the dating game. People say that the best way to find your life's love is to stop looking for it.

Do you believe in this?

If you do then you are on the right track. Trying to force attraction to someone you just met will only hurt you. The good news is that there's a way to find the "ONE."

It's called the *"5 Stages of Dating."*

We know what you are thinking, *"I gotta evaluate my level of likeness?"*

Imagine this — you meet someone in a club and you both immediately hit it off. Things are going great and you spend the night dancing and drinking. One thing leads to another and you both end up in bed. With one "don't" already done, you decide to see how things go in the morning. There's the awkward walk of shame and you don't call each other the next day. On the weekend, you make the call and ask the person out on a date and they agree. You go to a 5-star restaurant and as soon as you take your seats and the waiter leaves, you don't have anything to talk about. It seems like the charged atmosphere of the club, the booze, and sex dulled your senses and replaced attraction with lust. You never got the time to truly know each other, which is why you are now awkwardly looking at each other.

So, how do you know when you have met Mr. Right or Ms. Right?

Let's find out:

Stage 1 – Initial Meeting

Attraction

What is meant by the term "attraction?" It's when someone likes you for a reason. It could be your personality, the way you talk, the way you are dressed, etc. For attraction to take its natural course, you need to express yourself honestly and at the same time, make sure that you are talking about yourself in a positive light. This can be a little challenging because words can be misconstrued, leading to your date forming an unbiased opinion.

Attraction for Women

One misunderstanding that most women have is that men should talk the way they do. When a woman speaks, she expects the man to listen and ask questions to show her that he is truly interested. On the other hand, when a man speaks, he becomes passionate while talking, thus ignoring the woman. Keep in mind that this is something not all men do.

A woman on her date should talk more so that she appears more interesting. She should refrain from discussing her life problems because this might make the man feel that it's hard to please her.

Attraction for Men

To attract a woman, a man should do something that makes her feel special. A gesture as simple as complimenting her, noticing her a certain way, or making eye contact will work like a charm. These gestures should come without any expectations. If a man is truly interested in his date, these gestures will come naturally. Men are attracted to women who seem fun. So, get to know about your date's interests and hobbies to find out if there's any compatibility or not.

You probably expected things to go smoothly, right? Well, every situation has a challenge and so does the first stage of dating — it's expressing your attraction. The rule of attraction is that a man should do all the chasing and a woman should let him. However, the world is changing and if you are a woman who likes to take the lead then there's no harm in doing the chasing.

Stage 2 – Curiosity

Infatuation

In the second stage, you develop a sort of infatuation with your date. Not the kind where you stare at them creepily because, in your mind, you are plotting to tie them to your "YOU" style. You simply want to learn everything about them, because you are attracted to them. In this stage, attraction is related to physical attributes such as outward appearance and body type. They say, "Don't judge a book by its cover," but that's what most people do at this stage. However, curiosity is more than about looks. It's about getting to know each other such as likes, dislikes, hobbies, interests, habits, and more.

At this stage, couples seldom fight because if they see a difference in their date they don't like, it's dismissed with a thought like "she will change" or "it's not a big deal." Since you are trying to put your best foot forward, many things are overlooked. You might find yourself asking, "What can I do that will make them happy?" instead of "Are they the one?"

Uncertainty surrounds this stage because there are hidden depths to your date, and you want to peel them back one by one like the layers of an onion. This stage determines whether your date will become your partner or not.

Infatuation for Men

One question that infatuated people often ask themselves is whether they should pursue a relationship with their date or not. Infatuation blinds you to the important things in plain sight. A man may feel uncertain for various reasons such as is he the right man, does he care for her, do I like making her smile, and have I missed her since our first date?

If a man can't answer these questions, he might find himself stuck in the dating cycle and become a serial dater.

Infatuation for Women

For women, infatuation is an entirely different thing. Most of them tend to fixate on the future rather than the present; of course, this is not true for all women, but, in my experience, it is true for most. A woman's uncertainty stems from the worry that she might do something wrong and the guy will pull away. She watches things like a hawk in Stage One. If the guy gives mixed signals, the woman feels the need to chase him, and this is where she might end up sabotaging the relationship.

At this stage, a woman might make one of the following mistakes:

- After much hesitation, she will ask, "Where is this relationship going?"
- She puts in extra efforts to win over the guy, but they come off as too pushy

A woman's constant attempts might make him feel like less of a man, which will cause him to lose interest.

Infatuation Challenge

In this stage, the most important thing to recognize is the intensity of your infatuation, which is caused by uncertainty. A man might drift from one woman to another, whereas a woman might give her ALL to pursue the man. It might sound difficult, but you still need to go at a slow pace to make sure that you don't mess up the relationship before it even begins.

Stage 3 – Exclusivity

Becoming a Couple

You met, had a chat, liked each other, and met for dinner next. You are hitting it off, and so far, things seem to be going well. After a couple of more dates, the big question is raised — are you ready to become exclusive?

Exclusivity is a need that every partner has. It speaks volumes about a relationship, like having no competition and exchanging love without sharing it. This stage starts with commitment and conversations about the relationship. Don't assume that if you are sexually involved then you are exclusive. At this moment, words speak louder than actions, and you will have to wait to see how things go. You can either approach the person yourself or wait for them to make a move.

The deeper the connection you build, the easier sharing will become. You will feel more relaxed and satisfied in the relationship. In this period, you will notice your to-be partner's flaws and weaknesses. If a cute habit irritates you and the differences reach a point where you don't see any compatibility, you need to take a step back and see the whole picture.

Every relationship has its ups and downs, especially one that is just starting. You will either complain about them or have a sit down to solve them. The path you choose is what defines your relationship and lays down the first stepping stone.

Being a Couple for Men

For men, exclusivity brings complacency. He assumes that he's done everything in his power to win his partner and now that she's finally his, he can stop doing things to attract her. People often say, "Every day should be Valentine's Day." The same rules apply to the honeymoon period, in which everything is new and sparkly. A man should continue to plan romantic dates and work as hard as he did the first time to catch her attention.

Being a Couple for Women

Most women operate on the assumption that if she and her partner are exclusive, it means the guy should start doing things on their own. A woman assumes that she doesn't need to give the guy any clue of what she's thinking or what she wants. Women are complex creatures and the mystery they carry with them is what attracts men. However, when this mystery continues even after commitment then the relationship starts to seem like a lie.

The woman should accept even the smallest gesture of a man with a positive response. Only then the attraction will bloom from both sides.

It's not yet time to relax because you don't want to become too comfortable. Everyone will tell you that it's the little things that matter. So, a man needs to keep being romantic and a woman needs to speak up and ask what she wants.

Stage 4 – Intimacy

Chemistry

Yes, let's talk about sex. Well, not really. There are different kinds of intimacies — emotional, physical, mental, and spiritual. You now know the basics about your partner, such as their likes and dislikes. So, you can finally move to the stage where you will relax and get to know each other on a more personal level.

Do not confuse chemistry with attraction and lust because it is more than that. It's about sharing your feelings, vulnerabilities, and thoughts. An emotional connection matters as much as a physical one. If it's only the latter, you won't be able to spend even a few minutes in the company of your partner.

Chemistry for Men

Men have a mental barrier in place that keeps them safe from emotions. Compared to women, they tend to cry less. This is why they need to understand that a woman will show her vulnerability more, and her emotions will be constantly rising and falling like *waves*.

One minute she will be happy and all smiles, and the next minute, she will be too overwhelmed by her feelings to give anything. When her emotions are haywire, it's a man's job to keep her from feeling insecure.

This is where what you learned in Stage Three comes into effect. Instead of trying to force her to share her feelings, do everything in your power to bring her back to normal. This means taking her out on a date, doing something fun together, and listening to her when she speaks.

Chemistry for Women

Men tend to act like an *elastic band*. They will get close when the mood strikes and then pull away when they feel they are going too fast. For them, intimacy is a scary thing because they think they are losing their freedom. Therefore, they often ask for distance; however, this doesn't mean the relationship has ended.

There's a theory behind distance that most women don't understand. If you know your man is the one who truly loves you, he will come back to you.

For example, Samantha and Daniel have been in a relationship for two months. They both met at an open house and bonded over the property's windows. They exchanged numbers and decided to meet for drinks. They immediately hit it off and planned to get together in a couple of days. Despite having a hectic job, they both always managed to carve out time for each other.

After a month, Daniel asked Samantha to move in with him in the same house they had bonded over. The moment was special, and Samantha thought Daniel was the one. As their relationship progressed into their fifth month, Daniel's job became more and more hectic. He started staying late at work and couldn't give Samantha the attention she needed. Whenever he came home, Samantha would ask him about his day and try to do something good for him, but all Daniel felt was annoyance.

So, on the pretense that commuting was becoming difficult, Daniel moved in with his friend for a few days, telling Samantha that it was until the project was complete. However, in reality, Daniel wanted some space. Now, when Daniel came home, there was no one to greet him with a warm hello or a kiss. As days went by, Daniel started to miss his old routine — the comfort food, the couch snuggles while watching their favorite TV show on Netflix, having pillow fights, and more. Soon, Daniel realized that the reason he was feeling restless was that he missed Samantha. So, at that moment, he packed his bags and made his way back to his home.

A man's testosterone levels bring on this change in the relationship. Since women seldom do this, it's hard for them to offer their support. Do not try to convince him to come back because that just reeks of desperation.

Chemistry Challenge

Every person deals with intimacy differently. A man might try to run away from it when things get too much, and a woman might chase him.

Stage 5 – Engagement

You met, got to know each other, fought, and stayed with each other… that's a real relationship in our book. The time has come to make the ultimate commitment, and that is engagement. You can now bind heads and think about the future.

Think of your engagement as a practice phase that will help you see what your life will be like when you get married. The two most vital pieces of advice are to make sure that your relationship doesn't die as it becomes big. There are a few lessons that you need to learn, like acceptance and forgiveness. We say that you beat your partner first by apologizing. They won't be expecting it, which will be a huge surprise for them. A woman's love can change a person inside and out.

Just take Damon Salvatore from the TV show *The Vampire Diaries*. Even when he was a dangerous vampire, his entire focus was on saving Elena. When Katherine entered the picture, he didn't give her a second thought because he was attracted to the good in Elena. He changed himself completely from a selfish, psychopath jerk to a caring and loving partner. By the show's fifth season, he was ready to sacrifice anyone to make sure that Elena got out of the situation unscathed.

Engagement for Men

Now that you have tied the love of your life to you, you will face the biggest challenge of all. The one thing that most men go through during the engagement phase is that their personality changes. Often women complain that they live with a different man than the one they used to date, and it's true. Changes do occur in men when something huge like this happens in their life. However, the key to staying true to yourself is not letting your love fade away. Women can sense the most subtle changes in a person. They have a knack for it, a God-gifted knack that men are clueless about. Men need to give their best at this stage so they, their partner, and the relationship can grow together.

Engagement for Women

Unlike men, women display their feelings in front of everyone. They want those to be acknowledged by their partner. Any problems that arise are due to their unrealistic expectations, which can shift the relationship's dynamics. If a man can't deliver what a woman wants, the relationship starts to feel like a burden. Hence, women need to understand their partners. Instead of waiting for a big gesture, they should stand by their side so that they can know their struggles.

Engagement Challenge

The engagement stage is not a sure thing; this is when the real journey begins to find whether there's compatibility and potential to take the relationship to the next level, i.e., the marriage altar. Partners assess each other and try to develop a routine in which they are both comfortable. They get to answer questions such as:

- Will they stand by my side when the chips are down?
- Will they agree to a compromise in a problematic situation?
- Will they support me in my time of need?
- Will they take my side in an argument?

All 5 Dating Stages should be respected and followed in order. Sometimes, partners skip some of the stages because they are too eager. This doesn't mean that the relationship won't take its natural course and won't complete the missing stages at one point or another. It's just that partners won't gain the right insight at the right time, which can make or break a relationship.

You need to understand that a man should pursue, and a woman should create opportunities for a little push. In a relationship, the woman is a jewel, and the man should give her the right setting and room to shine.

Discovering Your Myers-Briggs Personality

Have you ever heard your friends or someone you just met say a 4-letter abbreviation? Perhaps, you felt confused and didn't ask what they meant to save yourself the embarrassment. With the letter tucked safely in the back of your mind, you decided to check them out later and forgot.

Well, that 4-letter abbreviation is known as the Myers-Briggs personality type that identifies the preferences and strengths of a person. It was initially developed by a mother-daughter duo, Isabel Myers and Katherine Briggs, to discover the personality types of people. Today, organizations, dating services, and many other places use this model.

Officially called The Myers-Briggs Type Indicator (MBTI), this test reveals how a person processes information, uses it, and interacts with people and the world based on it. Though MBTI is quite effective, you need to keep a few things in mind, such as:

- The personality type you will get might not be 100% accurate
- Don't fixate too much on your type or let it dictate your dating preferences
- No personality type is better than the other. Every person has different weaknesses and strengths. So, no matter what abbreviation you get, make sure that you don't take it to heart
- Don't fit yourself into a box according to your abbreviation

Now that you know the basics of MBTI, let's take a look at the traits that make up the abbreviations:

1. *Extroverted (E) vs. Introverted (I)*

When you feel alone and need a charge after a hectic day, do you: Go out with your friends (E) or stay at home and watch Netflix (I)?

2. *Intuition (N) vs. Sensing (S)*

Which description explains who you truly are: You love theories, ideas, and imagining future possibilities. You enjoy symbolism because you are a dreamer (N) or grounded in reality, living in the moment, and are a doer and very detail-oriented (S).

3. *Feeling (F) vs. Thinking (T)*

When you are faced with a big decision, such as breaking up with someone or choosing where to go for college, what's your decision-making process: Do you think with your heart, consider other people's feelings and involve your emotions (F), or do you use reason and logic (T)?

4. *Perceiving (P) vs. Judging (J)*

When you have to attend an event or go on a trip: You are flexible, spontaneous, and open to ideas (P), or you plan, make firm decisions, and lay down the structure that outlines what needs to be done (J)?

The following chart categorizes the personality types by abbreviation and traits:

MBTI Chart

MBTI Type		
Personality Type	**Abbreviation**	**Traits**

The Inspector	ISTJ	Introverted – Sensing – Thinking – Judging
The Protector	ISFJ	Introverted – Sensing – Feeling – Judging
The Counselor	INFJ	Introverted – Intuitive – Feeling – Judging
The Mastermind	INTJ	Introverted – Intuitive – Thinking – Judging
The Crafter	ISTP	Introverted – Sensing – Thinking – Perceiving
The Composer	ISFP	Introverted – Sensing – Feeling – Perceiving
The Healer	INFP	Introverted – Intuitive – Feeling – Perceiving
The Architect	INTP	Introverted – Intuitive – Thinking – Perceiving
The Promoter	ESTP	Extroverted – Sensing – Thinking – Perceiving
The Performer	ESFP	Extroverted – Sensing – Thinking – Perceiving
The Champion	ENFP	Extroverted – Intuitive – Feeling – Perceiving
The Inventor	ENTP	Extroverted – Intuitive – Thinking – Perceiving
The Supervisor	ESTJ	Extroverted – Sensing – Thinking – Judging
The Provider	ESFJ	Extroverted – Sensing – Feeling – Judging
The Teacher	ENFJ	Extroverted – Intuitive – Feeling – Judging
The Field Marshal	ENTJ	Extroverted – Intuitive – Thinking – Judging

When you have answered the above questions, you will have the 4-letter abbreviation that describes you. Find your personality type and then read the following to find out what kind of person you are:

The Inspector

Your ISTJ abbreviation says that you are an incredibly hard-working, reliable, and responsible person who knows how to get the job done. You don't mince words and communicate directly, whether the conversation is about asking out your crush or laying down your feelings.

- Defining Qualities: Relaxed, blunt, hones
- ISTJ Types: Condoleezza Rice, Queen Elizabeth
- Habits: You always show up on time at a party
- Most Likely to Be Voted: Dedicated

The Protector

Your ISFJ abbreviation says that you are dedicated to the ones you love. You always notice when your friends are feeling down. You jump into an argument and try to calm down both sides so that things can be settled before they escalate. You are a wallflower and, therefore, anticipate others needs. You are the shoulder that people cry now and feel relieved.

- Defining Qualities: Warm, kind, watchful, humble
- ISFJ Types: Selena Gomez, Beyoncé
- Habits: You are mostly found hanging with your close friends at a party
- Most Likely to Be Voted: Everyone's Friend

The Counselor

Your INFJ abbreviation says that you are a rare breed. Less than 2% of the world's population is INFJs. Your most unique ability is that you can read people and usually know what others are feeling. You are deeply empathetic, caring, and kind, and your friends open up to you with their darkest secrets. Your vivid imagination makes you a private person but is also charmed by a well-placed pun.

- Defining Qualities: Deep, caring, creative, perceptive
- INFJ Types: Nelson Mandela, Nicole Kidman
- Habits: You are the person who stands in a corner and watches other people at a party
- Most Likely to Be Voted: The Perfectionist

The Mastermind

Your INTJ abbreviation says that you are the mastermind of MBTI. For you, life is like a chessboard, and there are lots of potential moves. You are reserved, and at the same time, intelligent, direct, and imaginative. Everywhere you see, there are numerous possibilities to improve on. You don't like the popularity game and attend a party only when you feel like it. You are extremely loyal and have varied interests. Around 2% of the world's population are said to be INTJs.

- Defining Qualities: Independent, direct, innovation
- INTJ Types: Jane Austen, Mark Zuckerberg
- Habits: You are the person who gossips and pouts with your BFF and then leaves the party early
- Most Likely to Be Voted: Valedictorian

The Crafter

Your ISTP abbreviation says that you are a lone wolf. In the MBTI system, you are a rebel with a laid-back personality. Everyone wants to be friends with you because you redefine the word "chill." No matter what time of the day or night, you are always ready to have a good time. Though you are not very emotional and rarely divulge your feelings, you are super supportive. You always show up for your friends in their time of need. You dedicate yourself to work 100% and pay attention to the tiniest details.

- Defining Qualities: Analytical, supportive, detail-oriented
- ISTP Types: Michael Jordan, Olivia Wilde
- Habits: You are the person who arrives in style at the party, i.e., late, and makes a beeline for the basement to play table tennis.
- Most Likely to Be Voted: Biggest Rebel

The Composer

Your ISFP abbreviation says that you have an artist's heart and a sensitive soul. You might be a bit shy, but your personality comes out in full force when you are in your element. Any area where you are allowed to show your creativity is where you excel. Although you like to do things alone, you are still warm, non-judgmental, and tender-hearted. You love people, and they love you.

- Defining Qualities: Free spirit, creative, warm
- ISFP Types: Michael Jackson, Avril Lavigne
- Habits: You are the person who creates the party's playlist
- Most Likely to Be Voted: Most Artistic

The Healer

Your INFP abbreviation says that you are quite the dreamer. Your passion burns bright inside you, and you place immense importance on your values. Your friend circle is wide, and you love traveling, reading, and learning about different cultures. At heart, you are a true romantic and careful about sharing your emotions with the world. You are knowledgeable, active, and charitable.

- Defining Qualities: Idealistic, friendly, altruistic, big dreamer
- INFP Types: Audrey Hepburn, Lisa Kudrow
- Habits: You are the person who asks people random and interesting questions at a party
- Most Likely to Be Voted: The Quirkiest

The Architect

Your INTP abbreviation says that you are the brainiest amongst the MBTI types. Your brain is forever working and what you want to know is what makes the universe tick. You look for the patterns so that you can explain a phenomenon and then analyze it. You love logic and know every detail about small things. You are interested in subjects such as sociology and philosophy. When you meet like-minded people, your whole body lights up, and you become animated. Despite all this brainpower, you still manage to be silly and quirky.

- Defining Qualities: Individualistic, smart, reserved
- INTP Types: Albert Einstein, Bill Gates
- Habits: You are the person who sits on the couch and tells their theories to whoever will listen to you
- Most Likely to Be Voted: Most Brilliant

The Promoter

Your ESTP abbreviation says that you are too cool for school. You are the center of attention in your social circle, but you have never boasted about it. You love hanging with your friends and are a bit of a daredevil. You are a sports fan and excel at a lot of things. You have this yearning to experience new things such as skydiving, scuba diving, mountain climbing, and more. What's great about you is that you do all this with your laid-back confidence, which makes everyone around you comfortable. During an unexpected crisis, you are more likely to step up, offer people hope and take charge.

- Defining Qualities: Risk-taker, friendly, perceptive, confident
- ESTP Types: Theodore Roosevelt, Madonna
- Habits: You are the person who starts the party
- Most Likely to Be Voted: The Coolest

The Performer

Your ESFP abbreviation says that you are a person who lives by the motto "Seize the day." Your enthusiasm is infectious and can turn any dull and drab situation into a party, where people will be rolling on the floor with laughter. You are energetic and love to entertain others and excel on the stage. Hence, many ESFPs are actors or have a similar profession. You are non-judgmental and want to live life to the fullest. Moreover, you want the same for others.

- Defining Qualities: Childlike spirit, perceptive, fun, enthusiastic
- ESFP Types: Will Smith, Katy Perry

- Habits: You are the person who can be found on the
    dance floor
  - Most Likely to Be Voted: Life of the Party

The Champion

Your ENFP abbreviation says that you are a social butterfly who
loves everything. Your varied interests make you want to roam
around and make new friends. You love reading books and want
to connect with anyone by making them feel heard, seen, and
understood. You want people to recognize their awesome
selves and know how to rally everyone for commitment, making
you a great leader.

  - Defining Qualities: Creative, energetic, supportive
  - ENFP Types: Walt Disney, Ellen DeGeneres
  - Habits: You are the person who helps introverts feel
    more at ease at a party with engaging conversation
  - Most Likely to Be Voted: Most Inspiring

The Inventor

Your ENTP abbreviation says that you are a fascinating person
and have lots of layers. You are a true innovator and see
possibilities everywhere. You always move ahead with the
question "What if>" and tear apart the system to find a
solution. You have a huge social circle and are always up for an
adventure because you love gaining new experiences. You are
the person who starts a debate, plays devil's advocate, and
comes up with wild theories and ideas. Your playful spirits
attract suitors like bees to honey, so beware; you might end up
breaking hearts.

- Defining Qualities: Charming, bright, innovative, creative
- ENTP Types: Steve Jobs, Robert Downey, Jr.
- Habits: You are the person who can be found charming everyone at a party and flirting with some
- Most Likely to Be Voted: Most Innovative

The Supervisor

Your ESTJ abbreviation says that you are a capable person, and there are only a few like you in the world. When a task is assigned to you, you get it done. You are great at organizing people, ideas, and data. You always know how to come up with a solution. Off the clock, you are a chill person. Though you are social, you don't meddle in other people's business. You give respect despite doing your own thing. Travelling is in your blood because it helps you destress from daily life problems.

- Defining Qualities: Accomplished, assertive, a leader, capable
- ESTJ Types: George Washington, Judge Judy
- Habits: You are the person who can be found snacking at a party after spending an exhausting week
- Most Likely to Be Voted: Most Driven

The Provider

Your ESFJ abbreviation says that you are a kind person who likes to make people feel at home. You are the first to step up for anything and lead the charge. You never disappoint your friends. You go the extra mile by baking cookies and inviting them for a sleepover. You keep your family and friends close and talk to children in the same manner as adults. Your heart is always on display to put a smile on anyone's face.

- Defining Qualities: Sensitive, supportive, giving, detail-oriented
- ESFJ Types: Martha Stewart, Taylor Swift
- Habits: You bring the most elaborate and delicious cake to parties
- Most Likely to Be Voted: Mother Hen

The Teacher

Your ENFJ abbreviation says that you are a passionate person. You are charming, bright, and charismatic. You excel at things easily and have lifelong goals. One secret power you have is that you can read what others feel. If you ever chose to change your career paths, you would make a great counselor. You leave everything at a moment's notice when your friends are in trouble. You inspire others with your words of encouragement.

- Defining Qualities: Dramatic, driven, goal-oriented, loving
- ENFJ Types: Tom Hiddleston, Jennifer Lawrence
- Habits: You are always locked in a passionate conversation with someone at a party
- Most Likely to Be Voted: Most Charismatic

The Field Marshal

Your ENTJ abbreviation says that you are the leader of the MBTI system. You have determination, grit, and drive to excel. You are easily the most capable and smartest person in a room full of people. Reason and logic are your shining points, and you know how to tackle a problem that presents itself in the middle of a plan. Most ENTJs end up busing or in politics. You are a supportive person and always ready to help someone in their time of need.

- Defining Qualities: Determined, persuasive, focused, smart
- ENTJ Types: Gordon Ramsay, George Clooney
- Habits: Giving out directions at a party and generally being helpful at a party
- Most Likely to Be Voted: Most Likely to Succeed

These dating profiles are not set in stone. They simply give you an idea about the direction you should be going if your personality matches any of the descriptions mentioned above. If you find yourself nodding while reading it, there's no harm in applying what's written

The Ultimate Dating Quiz

The one question that most people are concerned about when they enter the dating game is, "Do I have a chance with her?" Whether the person in question is your friend or someone you just met at a bar, there are dozens of variables in play.

Here's a story that will help you understand this:

Megan and Josh have been friends for a decade now. Their bond is unbreakable. They do everything together. They know each other's dating history and secrets. Every weekend, they get together at Megan's house, and they both cook a meal. The atmosphere is relaxed and chill — they play video games and watch a movie on Netflix while munching on snacks. After a pretty hard breakup and being single for 6 months, Megan plans to start dating again. While at work, she was scrolling through her Facebook feed when she saw this Tik Tok challenge where friends kiss their best friends to see if they would respond or not. The video sparks something in Megan, and she decides to give this Tik Tok a try. Keep in mind that Josh has never flirted with Megan or touched her in this way. When the weekend arrives, Megan prepares a special meal and dresses a bit fancy. She puts on light makeup and makes sure that it doesn't look like she's trying too hard. When Josh arrives, they go through the ritual of talking about anything funny that happened at work, eat, and then put on a movie. Halfway into the movie, Megan cuddles into Josh and slowly tilts her head to look at him. When Josh looks down at her and smiles, she sees the opportunity and presses her lips to his. Josh immediately freezes and pulls back to look questioningly at Megan. When she doesn't say anything, he smiles at her again, closes the gap, and kisses her as he means it.

The smile in this scenario was the invitation that Megan needed to make her approach.

This is what we are trying to tell you. Your chances with a girl or a guy depending on the signal they give you. The following quiz will help you decide whether you should pursue a relationship with the person you have a crush on or not:

Q1. Do they have a boyfriend, girlfriend?

No

Yes

Sort of. I think they like someone else

Q2. Do you think they like you in the other sense?

No

Yes

I haven't seen any signs yet

Q3. Do they stare at you?

Sometimes

I have caught them in the act

No

Q4. Are you hesitating to ask out this person?

No

Yes

I am too shy so maybe, yes

    Q5. Are they rude or kind to you?

They are nice to me

They make me laugh

They talk to me rarely

    Q6. Have you ever heard them talking to their friends about you?

No

Yes

I have caught a few snippets but they always go silent when I come near

    Q7. Do they make an effort to talk to you?

No

Yes

It's mostly me looking for an opening

If your answers are "Yes" or "Maybe," there's a chance for you yet. You might not get the response you were hoping for, but it will be better than wondering about the possibilities. Dating is all about taking a chance because unless you open up yourself, you won't experience what life has to offer. Yes, there are equal chances of getting rejected and heartbroken, but you will *know*.

Dating Advice

A successful dating experience begins with you, which is why you need to focus on yourself. You need to be confident… ooze it even if it's the last thing you feel. The only question that you should be concerned with is, "Am I ready to date?"

Dating is about getting involved emotionally and, at a later stage, physically. If your past relationship didn't go well and left wounds on your heart, you might not dive fully into the dating pool. You can't float on the surface because that isn't fair to the other person.

If you have been away from the dating scene for a while, you have a blank slate on which you can write a new story. So, are you ready to find love and be a part of an awesome story along the way, which you can tell your kids and grandkids in the future?

At this moment in time, think of dating as an emotional apex. It defines the way you act, feel, talk, walk, sashay, dish the dirt, and flirt while trying to attract someone. So, right off the bat, you need to be clear on who you are. If you can't figure yourself out, how do you expect to find out what you want from life?

Writing Your Dating Story

You alone are the author of your dating experience, so take a look at your dating patterns, tendencies, desires, needs, and don't you dare gloss over the past boos-boos because they matter the most. Sure, in the fourth season of *The Vampire Diaries*, Stephen Salvatore became a villainous ripper when he realized that Elena was in love with Damon. However, you shouldn't indulge in psychotic behavior after a setback. We don't mean this as disrespect because every person has that self-destructive devil sitting on their shoulder, waiting to go on a bend and do things they will regret later.

The point is that you need to keep your eyes wide open while going on a date because a bad one will either be your fault or the person sitting across from you. One of the best things about self-awareness is that it brings power, action, and the potential for fun because you have a plan in mind. You know what you are getting into, and this will stop the guilt from settling in.

Your dating story depends on one thing, and that is a good conversation. It's what leaves a lasting impression and makes you memorable in the eyes of your date. The foundation of a good conversation is the ability to go beyond small talk. Sadly, this seldom happens because most people are nervous. Yes, you might be confident, but the struggle to appear interesting in front of your date makes you stumble over your words.

Instead of going to a 5-star restaurant, why not pick a place that is not too crowded but has a child-like atmosphere. Next up is relaxing and making your date feel comfortable so that conversation keeps flowing.

Here are a few tips on how to make a lasting impression on your date with a good conversation: Tips on Conversing with Your Date

Focus on the Conversation

At the beginning of your date, your thoughts might be somewhere else. You might think you are a good listener with the proper verbal and facial cues, but to continue the conversation, you need to take interest.

Why is it that you feel comfortable when talking to friends and know what to say next? Because you are genuinely listening to the conversation and trying to come up with the best response! So, relax and listen to what your date is saying and respond effectively.

The more vocal you are during the conversation, the easier it will become to talk about everything and anything. This doesn't mean that you don't give your date any room to speak. Just make sure that you both are on the same page. Your date might be an introvert so that they won't talk about themselves, but they might love listening to you.

Ditch the Questions and Make Statements

Here's a tip that will change your dating game.

Have you ever thought that questions put a pause to your conversation once answered? For example, you ask your date, "Where are you from?" They answer with, "Boston," and that's it. Now you are struggling to develop a question that will keep the conversation going with more than just a word.

Questions are not only boring, but they put too much pressure on you, as well as your date. Basic etiquettes of dating are that if you ask the question, they have to ask one too, or you might feel that your date is not interested.

So, what you need to do is make statements. Instead of asking, "Where are you from?" Why not begin with, "You look like a Boston guy/girl." This opens up room for your date to tell you a story about where they grew up. This is not a guessing game, so don't feel embarrassed when you are wrong. Simply follow up with, "So, where are you from?"

As mentioned earlier, what stalls a conversation is when you think about what to say next. What you need to do is listen closely and pick the hook points. Let's take the above example, you say, "You look like you grew up in Boston."

Your date responds with, "Actually, I am from Pennsylvania and grew up on a farm. I moved to Boston 5 years ago."

You have two hook points here: Pennsylvania and growing up on a farm. Talk about something cool that you have seen in Pennsylvania or recall any memory of you on a farm or a conversation on it with your friend.

To keep the conversation flowing, you need to note what your date says and then branch off by connecting to anything interesting. This way, you will never have any awkward, silent gaps.

Ask About Things You Care About

Let's say that you love traveling and exploring landmarks. This is something that you have been doing for a while. So, start your conversation there and see if your date is interested in what you are saying.

If you talk about something boring, such as what you do at work, you will bore your date to sleep. Also, don't make your questions sound like an interrogation. The line of conversation you start will set the foundation and will make your date open up. Make sure that your questions are thought-provoking and not just general ones so that your date can take part in the conversation.

For women, men need to ask questions that allow them to talk about themselves, such as, "What kind of music do you like? "Do you like long drives?" etc.

On your first date, keep your questions light. If you ask personal questions, be prepared to expect the same from your date.

Have an Opinion

Always speak from your heart. Don't just agree with your date for the sake of agreeing because that will make you look like a jockey or a dumb blond, and you know whats the joke on them. The fire in you is what attracts your date. So, you need to express your opinions and beliefs but not force them on your date or fight with them on theirs.

Don't start an argument because that will end your date even before it begins. Just don't be afraid to voice your opinions because you "feel" that your date might not like it. If they don't, they are not the right person for you.

One of the greatest pieces of dating advice you will hear from everyone is to *maintain eye contact*. Your smile and greeting will hook your date in. To get yourself to be more social, try practicing with other people, such as saying "Hi" to the barista you buy coffee from every day, the guy standing next to you in the elevator, the woman behind you in a line at the bank, etc.

It would be best if you swallowed your fears of putting yourself out there. We understand that it's easier said than done, but you will be stuck with your stutters unless you make an effort. So, next time when you go to your gym and approach the first guy you like. See how things go from there.

Conclusion

Dating can be a fun, scary, challenging, and exciting experience, but above all, it can be a wonderful moment in your life where you say, "I have found the one." No one ever said that dating is easy because finding someone who connects with you on some levels and enjoys the same things as you is not exactly a walk in the park. They also say opposites attract, so you never know.

Dating has many ups and downs, but they can be crossed by simply being your authentic self. Alright, so you do need to smell nice, be a responder, not get offended, accept your flaws and make them wait. We could go on and on with dozens of pieces of advice like this, but the only thing you need to remember is that look for that one quality, which makes you go, "This was great. Why don't we meet again when we are free to take things further?"

Ending a date is a crucial part of the process, and how you act and what you say have a huge impact on both of you. Never lead someone on if you didn't connect with them. You are wasting your time and giving them false hope about one single date turning into a relationship.

If you are not up for a second date and they ask you for one, smile and say, "I had a great time, but I don't see this going anywhere. Hope you find one. Good luck."

Bibliography

John Gray, (2018), _5 Stages of Dating_, Mars Venus

Sally Connolly, (2011), _The 4 Stages of Dating Relationships_, Mental Help

Sally Connolly, (2011), _The 4 Stages of Dating Relationships_, Mental Help